Also By Donald W. Grant

POETRY

Shades of Life

Echoes of

Life

A Collection of Poems

By
Donald W. Grant

DC

D2C Perspectives

ISBN: 978-1-943142-23-1

Table of Contents

Introduction

There are questions about so many things in our lives that seem to never be answered. Questions that have been asked probably since the beginnings of society, that echo over the years. Deep questions such as - Is there life after death? Why is there so much suffering? Why can't we just get along? This is a collection of thoughts, not to answer these age old questions, but hopefully to stimulate reflection on them. We do not always take the time to seek the truth, respect others' opinions, or look deeper than the surface of those around us. My hope is that at least some of what I have written will cause you to pause and hear the voice of the universe that echoes back to us, if we will just listen. Interspersed among the heavier poems are my experimentations with haiku. And a few tongue-in-cheek humorous poems.

D.W. Grant

Optimism

Early morning rise,
Before the light conquers dark,
Possibilities.

Silently She Cries

She stands taller than Helios,
"Keep your storied pomp,
Your conquering power," she says.
She calls out with a silent voice.
She calls to those who are poor,
She calls to those who are tired,
Calls to the homeless, the wretched refuse,
Those tempest has tossed.

They answer her call.
Je suis la, Я здесь,
Lo sono qui, Ich bin hier.
They come with hope, with dreams.

She watches as they strive,
As they blend and succeed.
She lifts her lamp, proud
And pleased at what she sees.

They soon forget the lands they left.
Their foreign tongues of how they spoke.
United they cry, "We are here!"
But to the lady their backs are turned.
New voices cry out, "Estamos aqui, vengamos!"

The lady has grown old but yet she says,
"Let them in, they are as once you were."
But they say back, " We will not, let's build a
wall."

A Truth Hidden

Like a shark gliding beneath the surface,
It fin hidden from sight.
Trying to remain unseen, yet deadly once
revealed.

Thoughts going unexpressed,
Actions kept at bay.
Glances quickly taken,
Lips staying sealed.

Laws have been passed,
Promises have been made.
Outwardly all is fine,
Inwardly there is no deal.
Man looks down on man,
Based on the color of his skin.
Racism is alive and well,
Bigotry and hatred are real.

We Have Become Numb

We have become numb to this.
Nine lives lost yesterday.
One lone gunman simply took them away.
Nine souls whom loved ones will now miss.
The cry goes up, "We need gun control!"
The echo back wails,
"My rights are protected!"
Laws that should be passed are simply rejected.
Only tears are shed for each lost soul.
Nothing changes. Names are added to a growing
list.
Killers are killed, some for life put away.
Memories fade. The lives remembered less each
day.
We have become numb to this.

Mediocrity Acccepted

Mediocrity accepted.
Sub-standard the norm,
Excellence becoming rare.

Apathy abounds,
Decisions go unmade,
No one really cares.
Classics ignored,
Taste out of style,
Acceptance of the inane swells.

Quality deteriorates,
Popular means third rate,
Extraordinary just a shell.
The question begging to be asked,
Will this be too much to bear?
No end in sight? No one can tell.

Opinions

You have yours and I have mine.
Although they differ and eye to eye we do not see,
Can we at least agree to disagree?
When did differences escalate to hate.
Have we gone too far?
When did we separate?
Once we could talk, argue, and debate.
Discuss with open minds
And at times compromise.
Now we just shout, we can't tell the truth from the lies.
Imagine if I listened to you,
You listened to me.
Could we solve the world's problems if we could just agree.
I don't have the answer but one thing I know
If we keep on this path there will be no place to go.

Facts Are Facts

Facts are facts.
Lies are lies.
You tell yours,
I'll tell mine.
At least with rhetoric
Nobody dies.

What is said, is
Often not what is heard.
A mouth speaks, an
Ear hears, somehow the
Meaning is blurred.

A question is asked,
A response is given,
Not to the question asked
But to the speaker's vision.
The ones that agree fail to take into account the
facts, the truth, the reality.

Instead, they mock, they scorn any who disagree.

Divisiveness reigns, agreements are few.
No consensus is found,
This is nothing new.

For years a gap has formed,
A wedge pounded in place.
The agenda has been met
To humanity's disgrace.

Red or Blue

Red or blue, does it matter to you?
Whether one is an elephant or one is a mule?
Do we need to pick a side, or just use our
differences as fuel?

So we yell and we debate.
No agreement is made, we just continue to hate.
No one can tell who might be right who might be
wrong.
Neither can give up the fight,
No one can just get along.

While we each stand our ground,
On the foundation we've laid.
No middle road is found,
No progress is made.
From the outside looking in,
To the world, we are foolish men.

The joke is on us
If in God we trust.
For 'til we can get along, 'til we can agree,
God wants nothing to do
With any of us.

The Blank Slate

Carson is an idiot,
Trump is a clown,
Looking at the candidates,
One cannot help but frown.

Bush is illiterate
Christie's a crook
Neither worth giving
A first, nor a second look.

Fiorina is delusional
Huckabee doesn't have a prayer
Would not vote for any of them
Even if they ran for mayor.

Hillary is too entrenched
Sanders never smiles
The list from both sides seems
To go on for miles.

Where is a leader when we need
One the most?
Seems all the good ones are dead,
Maybe I should vote for a ghost.

Words

Words are used, some are abused, some meanings
are lost.
Words get twisted, some get forgotten, some get
tossed.
Some say they go by the Word, but they act as if
they haven't heard.
They hear only some of the words, using words
like a curtain.

Using words like righteous, faithful, and pure.
Believing they are better for sure.
Believing they alone are certain.

The Word is used for hate, not love.
They claim their Word came from above.
They claim the Word is the only path to
redemption.
Sadly, one day they will hear the Word say,
"What a gross misinterpretation!"

Think Again

Without you guiding me I cannot kill.
To hold me in your hand gives you such a thrill.
My life is spent quietly put away.
Saving all my strength for that special day.
That day when you feel you are under threat.
The day you know is coming. It's just not here
yet.
So all alone in my box I lay in wait.
Hopefully, you have me placed where I am safe.
You fear that they may come and take me away.
You have no right to own me, they will say.
It is sad that in this world I need to exist.
But as long as I am needed, you will insist.
You paid a price, money
You have spent.
Too bad you misunderstood the Second
Amendment.

Rich Man, Poor Man or Them and Us

They sail on their yachts,
We look for things on sale.
They play golf at Pebble Beach,
We go to the beach, it's free.

They live in houses, huge and extravagant,
We struggle just to pay the rent.
They have maids, nannies, and gardeners,
We pay our kids a penny a weed.

They drive BMWs, Jaguars, or Porsches,
We are lucky to have a Toyota Yaris.
They get millions for ruining companies,
We get told you're no longer needed.

They don't have to worry about health care,
We get told you're no longer covered.
They don't seem to feel guilty or sad,
We don't understand, we get mad.

They act as if they don't even care,
We stand and watch, to them we aren't even
there.
Is this the way it was meant to be?
The haves and have nots miles apart.

No, this is not how it should be.
A revolution is about to start.

Myth?

Some say it is a myth
Some call it hype.
A myth is a female moth
Hype is just hype.
The word is used loosely
Tossed easily about.
Those who have not had one, have nothing to
count.
Some live their life
never to meet,
The one meant for them,
The one meant to keep.

Maybe I am just lucky,
Maybe it was just fate.
But I found my true love.
I found my soul mate.

My Three Loves

Isis, goddess of Egypt
Whose name is ancient for throne.
Cleopatra, Queen of the Nile
Her name is forever well known.
Catherine the Great over Russia she ruled,
The most renowned.

Three females of the past who reign once again.
Reign over my heart, the humblest of men.

You see Isis and Cleo are felines of mine.
And as for Cathryn, she is my wife, for now and
all time.
These three have my heart, my body, my soul.
But Cathryn I love most, if the truth be told.

Growing Old

It's a bitch to get old.
Closer to when I might die.
So every day I cherish, so every day I try.

My body seems fit,
My mind is sharp
I watch what I eat,
Only healthy food in my cart.

So now I am on Medicare,
Plan A, B and part D.
So even less of my
Social Security do I see.

But I am not complaining,
Not a harsh word will you hear.
I have a good life and a
Woman, I hold dear.

A World in Crisis

A world in crisis
So many killed by ISIS
Who understands this?

Reflection on War

They told us to just believe,
They told us to just obey,
A matter of pride and courage they said.
So some of us went,
Some of us stayed.

Some who went were killed,
Some who went were torn.
Men and women were lost,
Their children would not be born.

The war was just,
It needed to be fought.
They lied to keep us there,
The lies they told were bought.
Sons were killed, daughters lost,
Fathers wept, mothers cried
Their loss came at great cost.

Those who stayed were left with guilt,
They were alive not among the lost.

The truth finally revealed,
The nation woke up.
The people cried out loud,
"We have had enough!"

Those sent came home,
Tired and worn,
Maimed and broken.
Some in boxes
For all to mourn

Lives lost, lives destroyed
Victory unreached.
What a waste,
The liars not impeached.

Heroes forgotten, medals never worn,
Heroes spit on, wishing
They were never born.

One would think a lesson learned
The war was lost in defeat.
Surely this was the last,
We would not repeat.

How naive we were to think this would be the
last.
It did not take long
Before again they asked.

They told us to just believe,
They told us to just obey.
A matter of pride and courage they said.
So some of us went
Some of us stayed.

Some who went were killed,
Some who went were torn.

Men and women were lost,
Their children would not be born.

The war was just,
It needed to be fought.
They lied to keep us there,
The lies they told we bought.

Will we never learn?
Or will it be for peace,
we will always yearn.

Too Little, Too Late

They lined the streets shouting, "Love Not Hate.
Their message was good, but a little too late.

The soldiers had gone, off to fight a war.
Many were wounded, many were coming home
no more.

Politicians sent the ones that were poor.
The rich found ways to bypass this war.

When the fighting was over and no one had won.
It was then the true tragedy had begun.

Those that had fought had to hang their heads in
shame.
Those that had fought had to take the blame.

No parades were given, no ticker tape thrown.

Uniforms were spit upon, no medals bestowed.

As great as the lives in war were lost.
Greater were the suicides the war would cost.

The nation that sent them to fight and die.
Now rejected them. "We will honor you", was a
lie.

Years would pass before the country would recall,
The sacrifice that was made, the soldiers got a
wall.

After years of bitterness and hate,
Just a wall was too little, too late.

I Walk Among You

I walk among you
But your eyes do not see.
You give me nary a glance for to you, I"m
obscene.

You want to ignore me,
Pretend I'm not real.
Your ears ignore my cry,
A plea for money, for a meal.

It is easy for you to pass by,
To turn your head away,
Why would you stop?
Why would you give me the time of day?

Your eyes cannot see, nor
Your ears hear,
The story of my life,

That brought me here.

For what you don't know nor seem to care.
It was not that long ago
I was over there.

Over in a land so foreign to
Your brain.
A land of dense jungle,
Mosquitos, and rain.

So while you pass me by,
As I am easy to ignore.
Realize it was I who fought your useless war.

Heroes

There is a word that is used much too quickly.
To most it is thrown at, it will never stick, really.
The word is hero and is often misapplied.
For the only true heroes, are those who have died.

Alone on the Beach

Gulls flying above,
Dolphins leaping with the surf,
Quietly I watch.

What If?

What if on Sunday morning, all the pews were empty.
The people were out feeding the homeless instead.
What if people made good things happen,
As living prayers, not just bowing their heads.
What if all the churches that sit empty all week,
Housed and fed the down and out, with food and a bed.
What if people did not just read the Word, but actually did what it said.
There would not be anyone homeless, there would not be any unfed.
Is this too much to ask for?
Is this too much to imagine?
I am thinking it is, and if you're not sure, just ask John Lennon.

Unhappy Holidays

Tis the season to be depressed.
November and December, months with little rest.

Thanksgiving means too much food, relatives and
football.
Christmas means shopping, finding gifts for all.

Television bombards with images of family and
hope.
While most of us feel left out,
Nothing to do but mope.

Stores put up displays, carols fill the air.
Credit cards get maxed, we spend as if we do not
care.

Stockings get stuffed, our bellies do too.

Turkeys get sliced, enough for at least twenty-two.

Gifts are given, gifts are returned.
We thought our gift was perfect,
Will we ever learn?

We think of those not here, ones who have gone on.
While we complain about those who are, wishing some of them had gone.

Soon it will all be over,
Tables cleaned, trees put away.
The New Year will arrive, with the promise of a new day.

So to turkeys, Santas, and champagne, we raise a toast.
May time sweep us past the time of year, we hate the most.

Xmas Truth

The three wise men were not there, but no one
seems to care.
He was not born in December, when exactly, no
one can remember.

The angels did not sing, "Hark to the new born
king."
The Magi were not named, for that we have myth
to blame.

And as for there being three, no one knows how
many.
He was not born in a manger, though Mary laid
him in one.
And as for a stable, barn or cave, scripture
mentions none.

The drummer boy was missing, the ox and the lamb too.
The one truth for certain, He was born a Jew.

So it is not surprising that over time the message was lost.
Peace, goodwill toward men, comes at a cost.

Liar

You said you changed hearts, changed from the inside.
I gave you my heart, nothing changed. You lied.
You said I could live forever,
That I would never die.
Now laying in my grave,
I can see, you lied.
You promised that your Word would always be true.
Oh, how I wish I knew
You lied.
My life was a mess,
You said, "Come I will give you rest."
You lied.
Troubles and sorrows kept on piling high.
You said, "Let me comfort you."
You lied.
My troubles are many, my sorrows are deep

My life is mess, I can only sigh.
You said, "My soul you would keep."
You lied.
So your word is not true
Your promises are false
Your comfort is missing
Now my soul is lost.
I gave you my all, I really tried.
If I had only known,
You lied.

Don't Ask Why

He said he died to forgive our sins,
He said he died to set us free.
What happened? What happened to you, to me?
Chains of bigotry and hate, keep us down.
Misery, suffering, and pain are all around.
Don't ask, "Why?"

He said with a word or a touch.
He could heal the blind, cure the sick.
Was it really a miracle, or a simple parlor trick?
Famine, disease, and hunger run rampant.
More starve than eat, across this lonely planet.
Don't ask, "Why?"

He said, "My peace I give unto you."
His message was love and harmony.
The world today is full of hate.
Wars seem to never cease, some kill others,
happily.

Don't ask, "Why?"

Even He, when nailed to a cross, cried out,
"Why?"
There was no answer, no message in the sky.
So either he spoke the truth, or told us a lie.
It doesn't really matter, just
Don't ask, "Why?"

False Prophets

Every year the prediction is made,
This will be the last,
Our time is at an end,
He is returning, be steadfast.

Every year He doesn't show.
"But all the signs were there!"
You hear them say.
"The world is more than we can bear."

Yes, He said there will be signs,
Signs to let you know.
But, He also said no one can predict,
No one will ever know.
So thank you false prophets,
Keep predicting year to year.
As long as you keep it up,
The end will not be near.

His Holiness

A man with a cross, white robe, and skull cap.
Words of love and peace, how we each overlap.
All are one, and to each be kind.
To save the planet we need to be of one mind.
Take care of the poor, distribute the wealth.
Do more for others, and less for yourself.
A man with a cross, white robe, and skull cap.
Eyes clear and soft as if just up from a nap.
The pundits cry out in fear and despair,
This man is a Commie get him out of here.
He preaches Marxism, heresy, and lies.
The man is a menace, a devil in disguise.
He needs an exorcism, or to be hung by a rope.
This man is a fake, he for sure, is no pope.
The hate that spews forth shows how little they
know.
His message is sound and not just for show.
If anyone should leave, the pundits must go.

Resolutions

For some unknown reason
We think at this time of the season,
That the solution to our problems is making a resolution.
So we sit ourselves down and
Come up with a list.
To correct all the things that
Last year we missed.
Maybe we are too fat, or maybe too thin.
So we plan to do better,
Maybe go to the gym.

We plan to make better use of our time,
Maybe go on a budget, count out each dime.
Or maybe read that book that has been on our shelf,
We bought years ago from the section on self help.

So with determination and new energy.
We promise ourselves this year, I'll make a better
me.
Our hopes are high, our
Motives sincere.
We promise ourselves,
This is the year.

Time will tell if we keep
Our convictions.
If not, there is always next year, and new
resolutions.

A Boy's Dream

As a boy I did not dream of being a fireman.
Nor a cowboy, astronaut, or policeman.
My dreams were none of these, of a different
bent.

I dreamed of being a priest, white collar and all,
Going from place to place wherever the Lord
above, chose to have me sent.

You see, a priest is the perfect disguise.
For I wanted to be a hit man above all,
Killing for money, but only the bad guys.

Two Boys, One Summer

What do you want to do?
I don't know, what do you want to do?
I don't know, what do you think we should do?
I don't know, what do you think we should do?
I don't know.

What do you want to do now?
I don't know, what do you want to do?
I don't know, what do you think we should do ?
I don't know.

Let's go to your house
Maybe we will think of something there.

We walked across the field with cut hay, dust, and
blackbirds in the air.
The hay smelled stale, the dust clung to our
clothes, the birds attacked from out of nowhere.

We said Hi to your mom and went to your room.
We had to think of something to do, to ward off
the gloom.
What do you want to do?
I don't know, what do you want to do?
I don't know, what do you think we should do?
I don't know, what do you think we should do?
I don't know.

What do you want to do now?
I don't know, what do you want to do?
I don't know, what do you think we should do ?
I don't know.

Twelve-O'-Five, Fifth Street

Twelve-o'-five, fifth street.
A garage rarely used.
This is where the group would meet.

Four budding musicians,
The fifth off to the side.
Struggling to play each rendition.

A drummer, two guitars,
A bongo player,
Music always sounding subpar.

Gigs to be found only rare.
Skating rinks, fashion shows,
Always, not many there.
Somersets they were called,
Dreams of more unfulfilled.
Their musical career simply stalled.

Route 66

Summer beckoned, we were in our youth.
Two young men whose country had given the
call.
Before responding, time enough for one more
ball.

Like Milner and Maharis, in a 57 vette,
We packed it up, we hit the road.
Two hundred and forty horses to carry the load.

A convertible top, hoping for sun, no rain.
We waved goodbye, to parents and friends.
Alabama bound, on the road with its twists and
bends.

Taking our time, never moving too fast.
We made it to Albuquerque where we stopped to
rest.
Filling our tank we were told a tire might not last.

Driving on 'till one got tired, switching off to stay
refreshed.
We made it to Texas, his turn to drive.
Little did we know, we were lucky to be alive.

A slight rain had fallen while we were asleep,
Enough to drench the road, to make it slippery
and quick.
The curve was not much, slower speed would do
the trick.

One thing we forgot, one lesson yet to be learned
The rear tires were slicks, not meant for tight
turns,
Meant for straight courses, with rubber to burn.

We started to spin, the brakes were tapped,
steering wheel turned.
Corrections were made, all seemed to be fine.

Then we started to spin, crossing the line.

Around we spun, now out of control,
A bridge up ahead, a culvert below.
Around we flew, and we went down so low.
Still spinning round, we came back up to the top.
The ground grabbed the old vette, we came to a
stop.
Not a sound was made, you could hear a pin drop.
We jumped out the doors, and looked at the mess.
The vette was shredded, the fiberglass torn.
We looked at each other, my friend looked
forlorn.

Neither had a scratch, not even a bruise.
But the vette was gone, never again to be used.
Lucky to be alive, yet we were not amused.
The trip was over, almost before it had begun.
Two young men who now only felt sick.
Standing together on Route sixty-six.

My Yearbook

"You're younger than you look," or so I have
been told.
When I look at my yearbook,
I think I have grown old.
Then I see old friends who post on Facebook.
Pictures of their lives, and
Now how they look.
My only reaction is simply, Wow!
They have lost their hair or gained a few pounds.
Some I knew, I would not recognize now.
Grey is the norm, faces are round.
I cannot believe the change they have gone
through.
Then I looked in the mirror
And the mirror looked back, and said, "It's
happened to you too."

Disillusioned

At sixteen I felt your hand upon my head.
I stepped out to the world and told them what you
said.
I carried your Word everywhere I went,
Hoping to save some, lead others to repent.
It didn't take long for disillusion to set in,
It didn't take long for me to stop saying, "Amen".
So I took a different path,
One leading to science, leading to math.
And for years I strayed wanting not to obey.
My life fell apart, tears where shed.
 So it was back to you I was led.
I tended your flock,
I preached your Word,
And was there, for their troubles to be heard,
Night or day, around the clock.

It didn't take long for disillusion to set in,
It didn't take long for me to stop saying, "Amen".

My life turned again, and to some it was a sin, but I said enough is enough.
To some it was wrong but I knew I was strong, so to the naysayers, I said, "tough."
So now the years have passed and I have realized at last in all of the confusion,
That life is simply an illusion.

Seacliff

Seals, Dolphins, and Whales.
Every day near the beach.
Close to almost reach.

Where Are The Readers?

Where are the readers who devoured Dickens,
Hardy, and Twain?
Who escaped to the worlds of Tolkien, Verne, and
Holmes.
Readers who read everything from Hemingway to
Paine.
Readers who love the classics, the great plays, the
poems.
Shakespeare has been replaced by Patterson and
Child.
Connelly and Kellerman, instead of The Call Of
The Wild.
No wonder the world seems to be in a mess.
Readers are not reading the best,
Readers are reading it seems less and less.

Our Modern Age

So I sent you an Instagram.
You sent me a tweet.

I messaged you on Facebook.
You sent me a tweet.

I called your cell phone.
You sent me a tweet.

Twitter da doo, twitter da dee
How can I get you to just talk to me!

The Social Dilemma

Happy birthday, happy anniversary, happy
wedding too.
All these events never happen to me. Only you.

You post your life for all to see, how happy you
seem to be.
Two hundred likes, a thousand tweets, but none
for me.

So many friends you know, so many places you
get to go.
At home I sit, nary an invite, no chance to say yes
or no.
So enjoy your friends, enjoy the events, enjoy the
retweets.
As for me there's nothing left my friend, but to
simply hit delete.

The Lesson

We learn so much when we are young.
To divide, to subtract, to sum.
We learn of the past, how the world has become,
Of people, places, and then some.

We learn so much when we are young.
To dissect, to examine, to categorize.
We learn to question, to write, to quote.
We learn by practice, by listening, by rote.

Yet, for all we learn when we are young,
We never learn the important song.
The song that should be dwelling in our hearts.
To love one another, and not be pulling each other
apart.
Somehow they forgot to teach us all.
How not to criticize, how not to think small.
So, for all we learned when we were young
The lesson lost will be our downfall.

To The Poets

Prose can be fun at times.
But as poets know, it is more fun to rhyme.
There are all kinds of poems
And they don't have to rhyme.
It is fun to write haiku
Or just about any line.

The trick is to find words unique, words, maybe
we don't often speak.
Once a poet gets going, words seem to just leak.

The muse can be a fickle bitch, leading you on
then leaving you hanging on the edge of the cliff.
The cliff of despair that echoes, "Are you any
good?"
But still you write, like you know you should.

So you toil over each line wanting each to be great,
Hoping to be like Keats, Byron, or Yeats.

Deep down you know
Each word is part of your soul.
So you put them on paper letting your story be told.
And when you are done
Nothing left to do but move on to the next one.

To Leonard Cohen

At the age of sixty-nine
I have done a lot, seen a lot
Over my lifetime.
So it is amazing for whatever reason,
That it wasn't until the second season
Of the True Detective show,
That about you I came to know.
They used your song "Nevermind",
As their theme and the words stuck in my mind.
When I asked around if of you anyone had heard,
The response was, "Oh, man,
Have you not heard of "Suzanne?"
So online I went and on your albums I spent and
on some books about you too.
It seems "everybody knows"
You as a singer and poet.
Was I the last to know it?

I thought I knew some things, but this put "a crack in everything," I guess I am not so smart after all.
Being a poet and a writer I want you to know.
You have been an inspiration making my own work grow.
As I listen to your songs, listen to your words,
My mind explodes with the things I have heard.
With a pen in hand I write down all I can before I forget even a word.
So to you Leonard Cohen, I say thank you, while knowing,
Your hat I will never fill.

The Weeping Willow

There are redwoods standing majestic and tall.
Japanese maples whose leaves drop in fall.
Pine trees lined up in a row,
Cyprus that came from where, no one really
knows.
The street is covered as nature meant it to be.
Except one house, one yard has only one tree.
A weeping willow droops,
Looking sad and forlorn.
In the backyard of a house from where a young
child was torn.

A Rainy Day

The wind howls,
The rain pours,
The sea rages on,
The waves roar.

The lightning strikes.
The thunder booms.
The trees bend.
Much needed water
Will make the flowers bloom.

Inside it is calm.
We sit safe and secure.
The fire is going
I can hear the cat purr.

With a good book in hand,
The cat on my lap

The warmth of the fire
Means soon I will nap.

So let the wind howl,
The rain pour
The sea rage
The waves roar.
Just don't come around
On a day like today,
Cause, I won't answer the door.

Flor de Las Antillas

A simple pleasure, meant to be enjoyed.
Like a fine wine, savored, and taken slow.
Some balk at the practice but
Having never tried, how could they know?
Crafted with care, brought from a foreign land.
Plucked from the fields, molded by hand.

One cannot help but pause, taking time to reflect.
Life takes on new meaning, problems disappear.
Cares seem not as important, worries are few.
Loved ones are more important, and are held
more dear.
It does not take much, these feelings to catch.
One only has one task, that is to light up a match.
For this pleasure is tobacco, a fine cigar.
A Toro to be exact, taken from a wooden box that
holds twenty.

With fine wine, after good food, with good friends.
A simple pleasure, one of my few. I don't have many.

To Trash, Or Not To Trash

They want us to eliminate bags of plastic.
To some, this seems a little too drastic.
They want us to recycle bottles and cans.
Some just spread them across the land.

They want us to limit our water use.
Some won't comply, they just refuse.
All of this is to help the environment.
Some say it is too much government.

We have been given multiple garbage bins.
Each designed to put our refuse in.

One for trash, one for recyclables, one for weeds.
Each designed for a special purpose, a special
need.

So the question becomes, is it too much to ask,
To separate one's garbage. Such a simple task.

When We Die

Sooner or later we all have to die.
Through the ages, the question has been, Why?
Why do we have to die, or when we die, do we
really die?
Is there a heaven or is there a hell.
Since no one has come back, how do we tell.
The only why to know for sure is to die.
It is a fact, like taxes and tides,
That each in their turn will have to reside,
In a coffin or casket or maybe an urn.
Time is in control, we each just have to wait our
turn.
We want to believe that something comes after.
Maybe it is torment in hell or a heaven with
laughter.
If there is nothing at all, does it really matter.
Houdini had said he would come back and let us
know. But the day he appointed blew right by and
he didn't show.

After three days it is written that Jesus rose from
the dead.
Is this really true as the Bible has said?
Unless He comes back we won't know 'til we're
dead.
Whether this is the truth or this is a lie,
We won't find out until we die.

So in the meantime while we wait.
We have some choices we are able to make.
We can choose to love or choose to hate.
You might wonder if we just die,
What difference does it make?

I don't know about you, but I am going to do all I
can,
To be kind to all, be it a woman or a man.
For after I am gone and they play my last song,
I hope people will say,
"Hey, this guy was okay!"